I0198917

TIME TO
COOK
With Billy

Comfort Food to Bring Together
Family and Friends

BILLY MORRIS

HOLON
PUBLISHING

Copyright © 2022 William Morris

All rights reserved. No part of this publication may be
reproduced, distributed, or transmitted in any form or
by any means, including photocopying, recording, or
other electronic or mechanical methods, without the prior
written permission of the author, except in the case of
brief quotations embodied in critical reviews and certain
other noncommercial uses permitted by copyright law.
For permission requests, contact the publisher at:

www.Holon.co

ISBN#: 978-1-955342-58-2

Published by:

Holon Publishing & Collective Press
A Storytelling Company
www.Holon.co

In loving memory of my mom,
Annabelle Virginia Rice

Mom and Dad sitting around and singing gospel hymns at my Aunt Anna's.

I DECIDED TO WRITE THIS BOOK in memory of my mom, Annabelle, whom I loved dearly. I can remember waking up in the middle of the night to the smell of turkey and dressing. She would put her special touch on everything that she would prepare. I remember my mom would make everyday meals like it was Sunday-after-church dinner.

She always made sure that when my dad would come home after a long day of work, he had a nice, hot, home-cooked meal. The first thing that dad would say when he sat down to eat was, "This is some mighty good eating!"

Growing up, watching my mom cook was what led me to my own career as a chef. To this day, I love cooking for my friends and family. I presently work as a chef at Proctor & Gamble in my hometown of Cincinnati Ohio, where I have received several awards for my work.

Here are some of my favorite recipes. I put these together for you to enjoy with your friends and family.

Made with love,

Billy

Made with
LOVE

Sides 1

Lunches 12

Entrees 28

Desserts 42

Sides

Steamed Cabbage 2

Baked Beans 4

Grilled Asparagus 5

Yummy Pasta Salad 6

Sour Cream Mashed Potatoes 9

Broccoli Salad 10

Steamed **Cabbage**

Prep Time: 15-20 Minutes	Cook Time: 30-45 Minutes	Yield: 6-8 Servings

Ingredients:

1 large head of Cabbage

1 White Onion

1 large Red Pepper

1 large Yellow Pepper

2 tsps of Black Pepper

6 cloves of Garlic, minced

⅓ cup Sugar

1 tsp Garlic Powder

1 cup Water

½ stick of Butter, diced

Process:

1. Chop up cabbage to desired size.
2. Julienne red pepper, yellow pepper, and white onion.
3. Place chopped vegetables in the pan. Pour water over cabbage, peppers, and onion.
4. Add black pepper, garlic, sugar, and butter.
5. Cover and steam on low heat for 30-45 minutes.

My Dad, William, (in the white suit) when he was 17.

Baked
Beans

| Prep Time: 15 Minutes | Cook Time: 45-50 Minutes | Yield: 8-10 Servings |

My special baked beans. I can't tell you how many of my friends and family have asked me for this recipe. Sweet and delicious, these beans are made with a twist! The epitome of comfort food, I make my baked beans year-round, and they never fail to cheer me up and put me in a good mood. I hope they do the same for you.

Ingredients:

6 lbs of canned Baked Beans

½ cup White Onion, diced

3 tbsps Yellow Mustard

½ cup Brown Sugar

⅓ cup of your favorite Barbecue Sauce

Process:

1. Preheat oven to 350°.

2. Pour beans into a casserole dish.

3. Add onions, mustard, brown sugar, and barbecue sauce of your choice. Mix well.

4. Bake for 45-50 minutes.

Grilled
Asparagus

| Prep Time: 15 Minutes | Cook Time: 10-12 Minutes | Yield: 4 Servings |

Ingredients:

3 bushels of Asparagus

½ cup Olive Oil

6 cloves of Garlic, minced

Salt and Pepper, to taste

Process:

1. Cut off ends of the asparagus and rinse with cold water.

2. Place asparagus in a bowl and drizzle with olive oil.

3. Massage minced garlic into asparagus and season with salt and pepper.

4. Put asparagus in a stovetop grill pan over medium heat.

5. Stir asparagus occasionally, cooking for 10-12 minutes uncovered. Then serve!

Yummy
Pasta Salad

| Prep Time: 20 Minutes | Cook Time: 10-12 Minutes | Yield: 10-12 Servings |

Feeling like something light on a hot summer's day? Try this pasta salad to get your taste buds going. This pasta salad is a perfect outdoor meal to eat with meat cooked on the grill or wrapped up and brought to the pool! No good barbecue or summer family gathering is complete without pasta salad.

Ingredients:

16 oz of Rotini

4 oz pack of Mini Pepperoni

2 ½ cups Italian Dressing

12.25oz can of Black Olives

½ a Green Pepper, cut (julienned)

½ a Red Pepper, cut (julienned)

⅓ cup Parmesan Cheese

2 tsps Garlic Powder

4 oz Feta Cheese

½ cup Red Onions, diced

Process:

1. Boil pasta, rinse and drain with cold water, and put aside. Make sure pasta is drained well.

2. Once the pasta is drained and cooled, fold in 2 cups of Italian dressing along with all remaining ingredients and let chill for 2-3 hours.

3. Before serving, add the remaining ½ cup of Italian dressing to pasta salad and stir to incorporate.

Me singing at a Halloween party in 1982.

Me (top row, far left) out with my band, The Chosen Few, on a photo shoot in 1983.

Sour Cream
Mashed Potatoes

Prep Time: 15 Minutes	Cook Time: 20-25 Minutes	Yield: 8-10 Servings

Ingredients:

6 large Russet Potatoes

1 cup Sour Cream

1 stick of Butter

½ cup Condensed Milk

1 ½ tbsps Salt

½ tsp White Pepper

2 tsps Garlic Powder

Process:

1. Peel potatoes and cut them into one-inch cubes.

2. Put potatoes in water, leave uncovered, and bring to a boil, cooking until tender.

3. Once you can pierce the potatoes with a knife with no resistance, drain potatoes and pour into a bowl.

4. Add remaining ingredients and whip until smooth and fluffy.

Broccoli Salad

Prep Time: 10 Minutes	Cook Time: 3-5 Minutes	Yield: 6-8 Servings

Ingredients:

½ tsp Garlic Powder

1 cup Cheddar Cheese

½ cup cooked Bacon, diced

1 cup Buttermilk Ranch Dressing

½ cup Red Onion, diced

3 lbs Broccoli Florets

Process:

1. Rise broccoli florets well and pat dry with a paper towel.

2. Bring a large pot of water to a boil.

3. Add broccoli florets, remove from heat, and let stand for 3-5 minutes. They should not be completely soft, but they should be a bright green color.

4. Take broccoli out of the pot and shock it by putting it into a bowl of ice-cold water. Drain.

5. Stir in remaining ingredients and serve!

Lunches

World Famous Chicken Wings 14

Italian Sub Sandwich 16

Yummy Turkey Burger 19

Four-Meat Pizza 20

Four-Cheese Pizza 22

Veggie Pizza 23

Breakfast Pizza 24

Turkey Chili 26

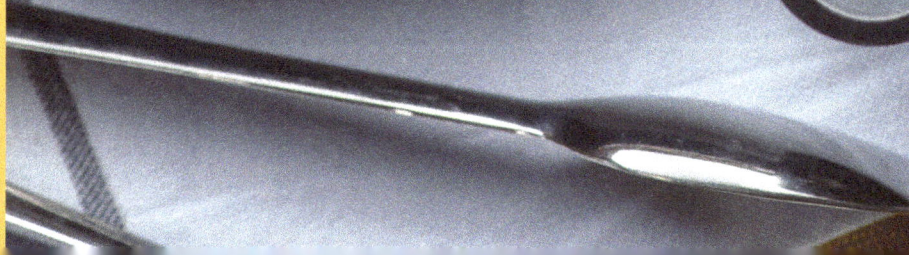

World Famous
Chicken Wings

Prep Time: 15 Mins./Overnight   Cook Time: 20 Minutes   Yield: 6-8 Servings

---

Perfect for game day with friends, gatherings with family, or just a simple night at home when you want something delicious and all to yourself, these wings never fail to hit the spot. Seasoned to perfection and golden fried, these are some delicious wings.

Ingredients:

12-14 Whole Wings

1 pint Buttermilk

2 Eggs, beaten

2 tbsps Black Pepper

3 tbsps Garlic Powder

1 ½ tbsps Paprika

1 tbsp Onion Powder

4 tbsps Seasoning Salt

3 cups Flour

Process:

1. Let chicken marinate overnight in buttermilk.

2. When you're ready to cook your chicken, add all dry seasonings to flour. Mix well and set aside.

3. Whip the eggs and put them aside.

4. Heat oil in a deep fryer or high-walled cast iron skillet to 350°.

5. Dip chicken in egg wash then dip in flour, being sure to cover the chicken completely. Repeat this until all wings are coated.

6. Gently place the wings into the oil. Make sure you cook your chicken in batches so you don't overcrowd your fryer/pan.

7. When the chicken starts to float, check the temperature. It should read 165° when done. If you don't have a meat thermometer, cook until golden brown.

Italian Sub
Sandwich

Prep Time: 5-10 Minutes	Cook Time: N/A	Yield: 4 Sandwiches

Ingredients:

12 slices of Honey Ham

12 slices of Salami

8 slices of Swiss Cheese

1 small Red Onion, sliced

4 Hoagie Rolls

½ cup Banana Peppers

4-6 leaves of Shredded Lettuce

½ cup Black Olives

2 large Tomatoes

Mayo, to taste

Italian Dressing, to taste

Process:

1. Lightly toast each bun.

2. Build each sandwich, starting with mayo, lettuce, tomato, red onion, black olives, and banana peppers. Then add 3 slices of salami, 3 slices of ham, and 2 slices of Swiss cheese to each.

My little brother, Corey, on his journey to California in 1998.

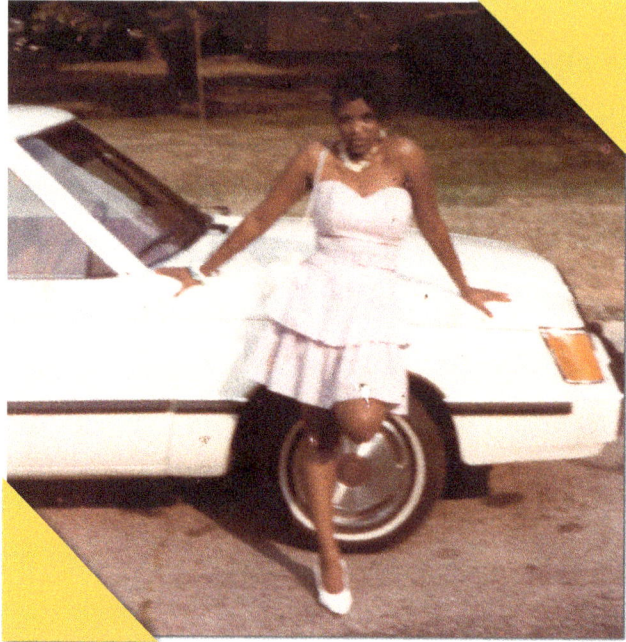

My sister, Pam, all jazzed up for the jazz festival.

Me (front, center) and my classmates at Scarlet Oaks Vocational School in 1979.

Yummy
Turkey Burger

Prep Time: 15-135 Minutes   Cook Time: 12 Minutes   Yield: 3 Burgers

Ingredients:

1 lb Ground Turkey

½ cup Bread Crumbs

1 ½ tsps Garlic Powder

½ tsp Salt

1 Egg, beaten

¼ cup White Onion, diced

3 Buns

1 Tomato, sliced

3-6 leaves of Lettuce

Process:

1. Combine all ingredients together in a medium-sized bowl. Mix until fully incorporated.

2. Form into 3 quarter-pound patties.

3. Place on wax paper and let chill in the refrigerator for 2 hours.

4. When you're ready to cook your burgers, heat a pan over medium-high heat and gently place your patties.

5. Sear them over medium heat for roughly 6 minutes on each side, turning occasionally.

6. Garnish with lettuce and tomato.

Four-Meat Pizza

Prep Time: 10 Minutes	Cook Time: 15-20 Minutes	Yield: 2-3 Servings

Ingredients:

2 ½ cups Mozzarella Cheese, shredded

12-inch Pizza Shell

1 pack of Pepperoni

8 strips of Bacon

2 links of Turkey or Pork Italian Sausage

½ cup Ham, diced

1 cup Pizza Sauce (see recipe below)

Process:

1. Preheat oven to 395°.

2. Squeeze sausage out of the casing and into a pan. Cook on medium heat, stirring and breaking up the meat until crispy and brown.

3. Cook bacon over medium heat, flipping occasionally until crispy on both sides. Dice once it is cooled.

4. Spread sauce on the pizza shell then add the remaining ingredients to your liking.

5. Bake for 12-15 minutes.

Pizza Sauce

Ingredients:

28 oz can of Tomato Sauce

1 cup Parmesan Cheese

4 tsps Oregano

4 tbsps Garlic Powder

Process:

1. Stir ingredients together, then use on your favorite pizza! This recipe can be used to make 3 12-inch pizzas.

Four-Cheese Pizza

Prep Time: 10 Minutes	Cook Time: 15-20 Minutes	Yield: 2-3 Servings

Ingredients:

12-inch Pizza Shell

2 ½ cups Mozzarella Cheese, shredded

⅓ cup Cheddar Cheese, shredded

⅓ cup Parmesan Cheese, grated

⅓ cup Provolone Cheese, shredded

½ tsp Oregano (garnish)

1 cup Pizza Sauce (see recipe on page 20)

Process:

1. Preheat oven to 400°.
2. Spread sauce on the pizza shell then add the remaining cheeses.
3. Bake for 12-15 minutes, or until done.
4. Sprinkle oregano on top for garnish.

Veggie Pizza

Prep Time: 10 Minutes	Cook Time: 15-20 Minutes	Yield: 2-3 Servings

Ingredients:

12-inch Pizza Shell

1 small Red Pepper, cut (julienned)

1 small Yellow Pepper, cut (julienned)

½ cup Red Onion, cut (julienned)

2 ½ cups Mozzarella Cheese, shredded

½ cup Parmesan, grated

2 cups Spinach, steamed

⅓ cup Black Olives

1 cup Pizza Sauce (see recipe on page 20)

Process:

1. Preheat oven to 400°.

2. Spread sauce on the pizza shell then add the remaining ingredients to your liking.

3. Bake for 12-15 minutes, or until done.

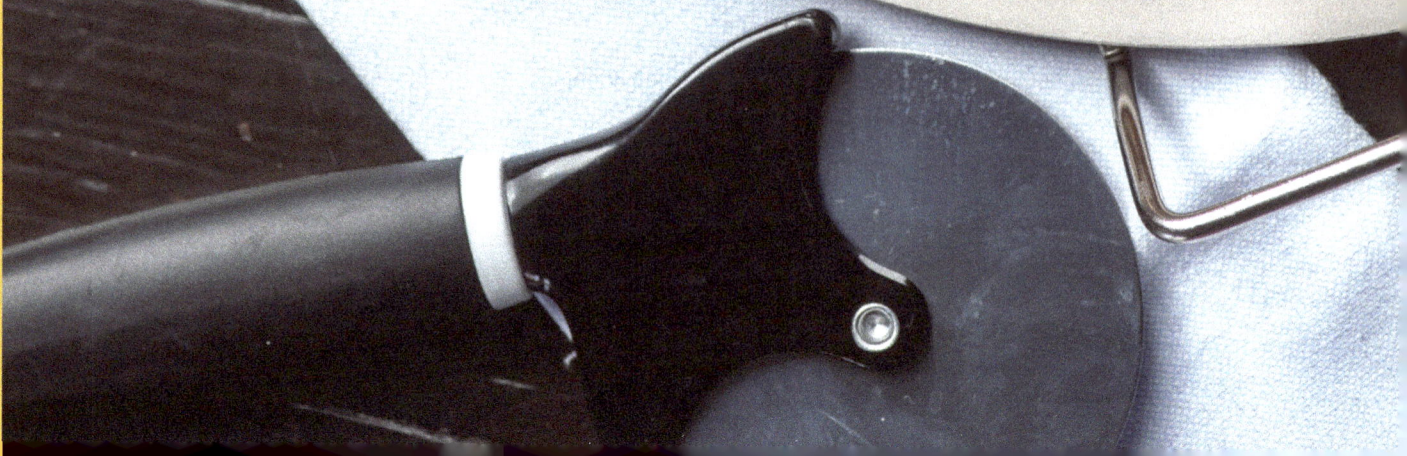

Breakfast Pizza

Prep Time: 10 Minutes   Cook Time: 20-25 Minutes   Yield: 2-3 Servings

We've all been there; it's a lazy morning, and you don't feel like cooking. You go to the fridge and find a leftover piece of pizza from last night. Sure it's a day old, and certainly not breakfast food. But doesn't that pizza just taste extra delicious when you eat it in the morning? My breakfast pizza is just that but spruced up a little. Complete with eggs, sausage gravy, and ham, this recipe is everything you love about breakfast combined with that perfect slice of pizza.

Ingredients:

12-inch Pizza Shell

15 oz can of Sausage Gravy

8 strips of cooked Bacon, diced

8 oz Cheddar Cheese, shredded

½ cup Ham, diced

6 cooked Sausage Patties, crumbled

6 Eggs, beaten

Process:

1. Preheat oven to 350°.
2. Scramble eggs and set aside.
3. Spread your sausage gravy evenly on the pizza shell.
4. Add cheese then scrambled eggs. Add remaining ingredients.
5. Bake for 15-20 minutes, or until done.

Turkey Chili

Prep Time: 10-15 Minutes   Cook Time: 90-120 Minutes   Yield: 6-8 Servings

On a cold day, nothing warms body and soul like a nice bowl of chili. This is the perfect snack to make for kids who have just come in from playing in the snow, or for you with a glass of wine in front of a blazing fire. Add sour cream and cheese to your heart's content and cozy up. I can smell the steam rising off of it already!

Ingredients:

2 packs of Mild Chili Mix

3 lbs Ground Turkey

29 oz can of Tomato Sauce

12 oz can of Tomato Paste

32 oz Bottled Water

8 cloves Garlic, minced

1 medium Red Pepper, diced

1 medium Yellow Pepper, diced

2 medium White Onions, diced

½ cup Sugar

6 tbsps Garlic Powder

15.5 oz can of Kidney Beans

2 cups cooked Macaroni

2 tsps Black Pepper

Process:

1. Over medium heat, combine garlic, peppers, onions, and ground turkey in a pot. Cook until turkey is golden brown.

2. Drain grease from the pot and add tomato sauce, tomato paste, 2 bottles of water, ½ cup of sugar, and kidney beans. Let cook on low heat for 35 minutes.

3. Add pasta and cook for another 45 minutes, then serve.

Me and my family funking around in 2017 at the Hollywood Museum in downtown LA.

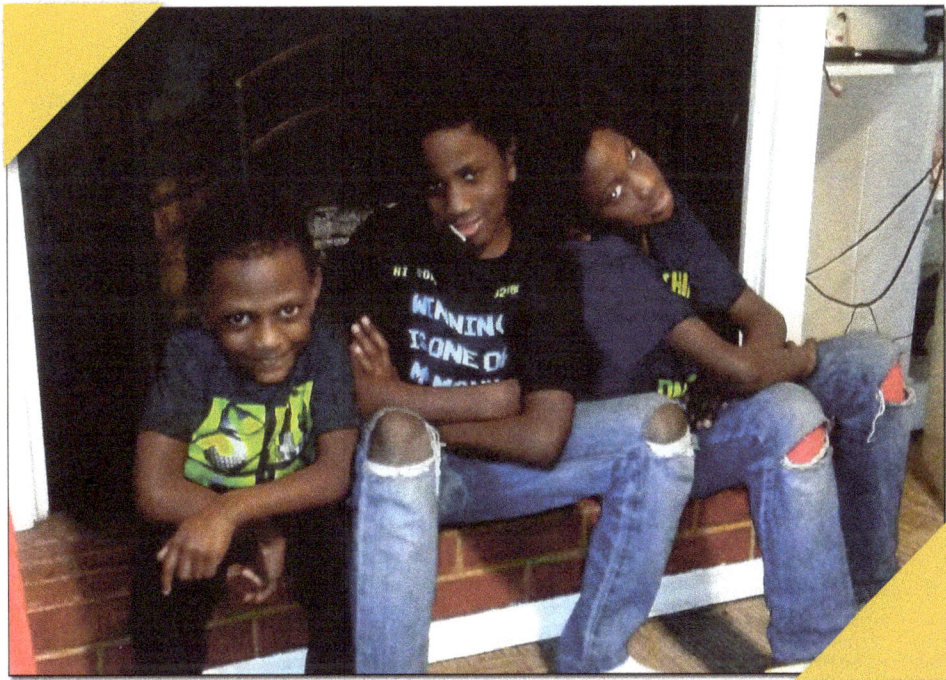

Having fun with the three amigos, Jayden, Jordan, and Jeremiah!

Entrees

Grilled Baby Back Ribs 30

Roasted Turkey 34

Corn Bread Dressing 36

Turkey Pasta Bake 38

Blackened Salmon *with* **Pineapple Relish** 41

Grilled
Baby Back Ribs

Prep Time: 25 Mins./Overnight   Cook Time: 180 Minutes   Yield: 6-8 Servings

Nothing says "summer" like getting out the grill and the smell of smoke and seasoning in the air. These baby back ribs are best served in the backyard with family and kids running all around. Smokey, savory, and downright delicious, these ribs are sure to make you the belle of the barbecue, and they will make your taste buds happy any time of year.

Ingredients:

2 gallon-sized Plastic Bags

2 Baby Back Rib Racks

16 oz Italian Dressing

6 tsps Garlic Powder

6 tsps Steak Seasoning

3 tsps Paprika

4 tsps Onion Powder

3 tsps Black Pepper

Process:

1. Rinse ribs with cold water and pat dry.

2. Using a paring knife, turn ribs over and proceed to remove the silverskin.

3. Place the ribs in large plastic bags and pour half of the Italian dressing into each bag. Shake it up to cover completely and marinate in the refrigerator overnight.

4. The next day, preheat your grill.

5. Take ribs out of the bags and proceed to season with steak seasoning, garlic powder, black pepper, onion powder, and paprika on both sides.

6. Grill on a gas or charcoal grill for about an hour and a half, continuing to turn every so often.

7. Preheat oven to 255°.

8. Cover with foil and bake for about 1 hour and 15 minutes.

9. Add your favorite barbecue sauce and enjoy!

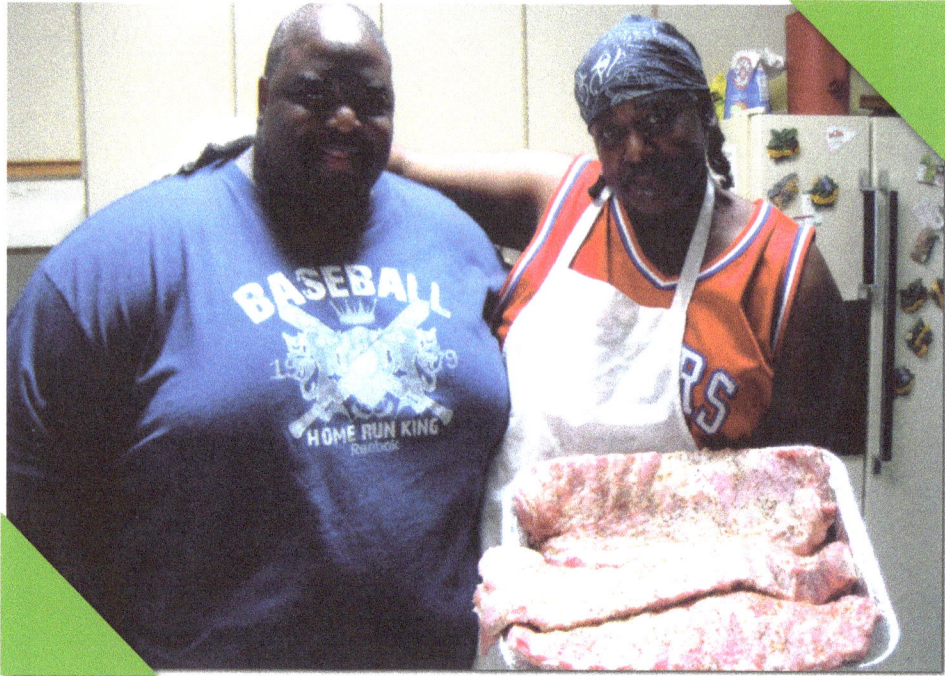

The Morris Brothers getting their grub on in August 2009.

Can't you just smell the aroma of baby back ribs?

Me enjoying the Hollywood Walk of Fame in beautiful California.

Roasted Turkey

Prep Time: 20 Minutes   Cook Time: 270-330 Minutes   Yield: 15 Servings

A good turkey makes a beautiful centerpiece, but it shouldn't eat up all your cooking time. Thanksgiving has always been my favorite holiday, but with so many delicious meals to make, I wanted a turkey that would be as efficient as it was delicious. I season my turkey with a variety of special spices so it comes out fragrant and delicious without having to sit for hours in a brine. This way, I can work on my stuffing and sweet potato pie and not be rushed for time!

Ingredients:

18-22 lb Turkey

1 stick of Unsalted Butter, softened

Black Pepper*

Seasoning Salt*

Poultry Seasoning*

Garlic Powder*

Onion Powder*

*Just have the entire jar on hand.

Process:

1. Preheat oven to 335°.

2. Remove giblets from the inner cavity of the turkey. Rinse the bird and pat it and dry with a paper towel.

3. Melt butter and rub it evenly over the entire outside of the turkey.

4. Sprinkle garlic powder, black pepper, poultry seasoning, and onion powder over the entire bird, breast side up.

5. Place sheets of foil over the turkey, securing them underneath the pan.

6. Bake for 4 ½-5 ½ hours, basting every hour.

7. Take the foil off for your last hour of cooking until golden brown all over. Temperature should read 165° when done.

Corn Bread
Dressing

Prep Time: 20 Minutes	Cook Time: 45-55 Minutes	Yield: 12-14 Servings

A savory blend of ingredients to make your mouth water on Thanksgiving—or any day. I would drink this dressing if I could. Perfect for turkey, chicken, potatoes, and more, this versatile dressing elevates your meal, even if it is just the back-of-the-fridge leftovers in March!

Ingredients:

Corn Bread

- 2 ½ cups Yellow Cornmeal (self-rising)
- 1 cup Flour (self-rising)
- 1 ½ tsps Salt
- 3 large Eggs, beaten
- ½ cup Olive Oil
- 2 ½ cups Buttermilk

Dressing

- 12 oz package of Sage and Onion Cubed Stuffing
- 1 ½ cups Celery, diced
- 1 ½ cups White Onion, diced
- 32 oz can of Cream of Celery Soup
- 32 oz can of Cream of Chicken Soup
- 48 oz carton of Chicken Broth
- 1-2 tsps Salt
- 3 tbsps Dried Sage
- 2 tbsps Garlic Powder

Process:

Corn Bread

1. Corned bread should be made the day prior and set aside. Preheat oven to 350°.
2. Combine all ingredients minus the olive oil in a large bowl.
3. Heat olive oil in the oven and pour hot oil into the mixture.
4. Pour mixture into pan and bake 45-50 minutes, or until golden brown.

Dressing

5. Preheat oven to 350°.
6. Take the corned bread and crumble it up in a mixing bowl.
7. Add remaining ingredients and stir mixture together until everything is well incorporated.
8. Pour mixture into a medium to large casserole dish and spread evenly.
9. Bake for 45-55 minutes or until lightly golden.

Turkey
Pasta Bake

Prep Time: 20-25 Minutes	Cook Time: 35-45 Minutes	Yield: 6-8 Servings

Ingredients:

3 lbs Ground Turkey

2 lbs Italian Turkey Sausage

6 cups Mozzarella Cheese, shredded

2 cups Parmesan Cheese, grated

16 oz Penne

¾ cup Sugar

2 tbsps Italian Seasoning

16 oz of Marinara Sauce

2 tbsps Oregano

1 Green Pepper, cut (julienned)

1 Red Pepper, cut (julienned)

1 Yellow Pepper, cut (julienned)

1 large White Onion, cut (julienned)

6 cloves Garlic, minced

Process:

1. Preheat oven to 350°.

2. In a skillet over medium heat, cook the ground turkey, breaking it into crumbles. In a separate skillet, do the same thing with the Italian turkey sausage.

3. Before the meat begins to brown, add the peppers, onion, and minced garlic to the ground turkey and cook until brown. Drain grease and transfer to a large bowl.

4. To the bowl, add half of the mozzarella and parmesan cheeses along with the sugar, marinara sauce, oregano, and Italian seasoning. Mix well and set aside.

5. Cook pasta, shock in a bowl of cold water, then drain.

6. Fold pasta in with remaining ingredients then pour into a large baking dish. Top off with remaining cheeses and bake loosely covered with foil so the cheese won't stick to foil. Bake for 35-45 minutes, or until cheese is bubbly and melted.

I just made a wonderful summer meal for my family and me.

Another summer day. Just food, family, and enjoying each other's company.

Having a wonderful day at the beach with Janine and Brandon in Santa Clarita, California.

Blackened Salmon
with Pineapple Relish

| Prep Time: 25 Minutes | Cook Time: 6-12 Minutes | Yield: 4 Servings |

Ingredients:

Salmon

4 Salmon Filets

16 tsps Blackened Seasoning

6 cloves Garlic, minced

½ stick of Butter

⅓ cup Olive Oil

Pineapple Relish

½ a small Red, Yellow, and Green Pepper

½ cup Red Onion, diced

1 cup Pineapple, diced

Process:

1. The pineapple relish is best if it's allowed to set up over night. Cut up a half of red, yellow, and green pepper and a half cup of diced red onion and a cup of diced pineapple. Let set up over night.

2. When you are ready to cook the salmon, melt butter in a skillet.

3. Coat each salmon filet with garlic and drizzle with olive oil.

4. Sprinkle each cutlet evenly with approximately 4 tsps of blackened seasoning. Cook over medium heat for 5-6 minutes on each side, or until cooked to your liking.

5. Top with pineapple relish.

Desserts

Bread Pudding *with* **Bourbon Sauce** 44

Yummy Sweet Potato Pie 46

Pineapple Pecan Cake 48

Banana Pudding Cake 50

Chocolate Cherry Pudding Cake 54

Bread Pudding
with Bourbon Sauce

Prep Time: 10 Mins./Overnight   Cook Time: 45-50 Minutes   Yield: 10-12 Servings

---

Ingredients:

Bread Pudding

  1 dozen Glazed Donuts
(best if stale)

  1 dozen Cake Donuts
(best if stale)

  3 cups Half and Half

  2 Eggs

  2 tsps Vanilla Extract

  2 tbsps Cinnamon

  ½ cup Chocolate Chips

  ½ cup Dried Coconut,
shredded

  ½ cup Pecans, diced

Bourbon Sauce

  ¾ cup Butter

  2 cups Brown Sugar

  1 ¼ cups Heavy
Whipping Cream

  2 tbsps Light Corn
Syrup

  ¼ tsp Salt

  2 tsps Bourbon

  3 cups Powdered Sugar

  2 tsps Vanilla Extract

Process:

1. Cut donuts into cubes and throw into a mixing bowl. To the bowl add coconut, chocolate chips, and pecans.

2. In a separate bowl, add vanilla, half and half, 2 eggs, and cinnamon, and mix until all ingredients are combined.

3. Pour mixture over the donuts and let sit overnight.

4. The next day, preheat your oven to 350° and bake the cake for 45-50 minutes.

5. Meanwhile, melt the butter in a deep, heavy-duty saucepan over low heat for the bourbon sauce. Once melted, increase heat to medium-high and bring to a boil. Continue to stir until butter is fragrant and starts to brown, about 4 minutes.

6. Remove the pan from heat and stir in the brown sugar, heavy whipping cream, corn syrup, salt, and bourbon of your choice. Return to heat and stir until all ingredients are combined, about 1 minute.

7. Remove from heat. Slowly add the powdered sugar a little at a time and continue to stir until it turns into a sauce. Add the vanilla.

8. Drizzle sauce over the bread pudding and enjoy.

Pineapple Pecan Cake

Prep Time: 15 Minutes	Cook Time: 25-35 Minutes	Yield: 8-10 Servings

Ingredients:

Cake

- 3 cups Flour
- 1 cup Pecans, chopped (reserve half for Icing)
- 1 tsp Baking Soda
- 2 tsps Cinnamon
- ½ tsp Salt
- 2 cups Bananas, diced
- 3 large Eggs, beaten
- 8 oz can of Crushed Pineapple (reserve half for Icing)
- 2 cups Sugar
- 1 cup Canola Oil
- 2 tsps Vanilla Extract

Icing

- 8 oz block of Cream Cheese
- 6 cups Powdered Sugar
- 1 tbsp Milk
- 1 ½ tsps Vanilla Extract
- ½ stick of Butter, softened

Process:

1. Preheat oven to 350°.
2. Whisk flour, baking soda, salt, cinnamon, and sugar together.
3. Add half of the pecans to the mixture. Add half of the crushed pineapple to the mixture and set the remaining aside for icing.
4. Grease and flour two 9-inch cake pans, then set aside.
5. To the bowl, add the eggs, oils, and vanilla. Fold all ingredients together.
6. Pour evenly in cake pans and bake for 25-30 minutes, or until done.
7. Combine all of the ingredients for the cream cheese icing. Add the remaining ½ cup of pecans and ½ cup of pineapple. Whip all ingredients together until smooth.
8. Let cakes cool, then spread on the cream cheese icing.

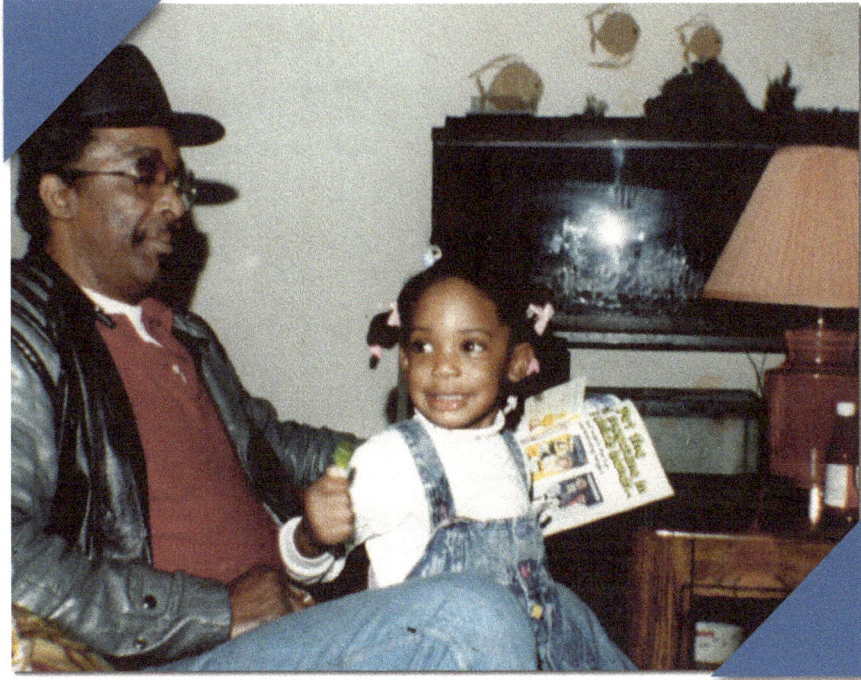

My Dad and niece, Ashley, having some fun together in 1992.

Just made a freshly baked Pineapple Pecan Cake for Aunt Anna and Uncle Solomon.

Yummy
Sweet Potato Pie

Prep Time: 30-45 Minutes   Cook Time: 45-55 Minutes   Yield: 2 Pies

As a child, my mom would prepare this sweet potato pie every Thanksgiving. Even though it has been years since my mom passed away, when I smell the aroma of cinnamon billowing through the house, I am brought back to the Thanksgivings of my childhood. This sweet potato pie is perfect to share with friends and family as you give thanks for all you have—or any time of year when you want to feel transported to simpler days!

Ingredients:

Potato Mixture

- **1 stick of Butter, softened**
- **2 tsps Vanilla Extract**
- **6 medium Sweet Potatoes**
- **2 Eggs, beaten**
- **1 cup Sweetened Condensed Milk**
- **2 tbsps Cinnamon**
- **1 ½ tbsps Pumpkin Spice**
- **½ cup Brown Sugar**

Pie Crust

- **3 cups of finely ground Graham Crackers**
- **12 tbsps of melted Butter (divided pie crust for 2)**
- **½ cup of Sugar**
- **1 tbsp of Cinnamon**

Process:

1. Preheat oven to 375°.
2. Peel potatoes and dice into one-inch pieces.
3. Boil until tender.
4. Combine all potato mixture ingredients together in a bowl and whip until smooth.
5. For the crust, combine all graham cracker pie crust ingredients in a bowl.
6. Press it into an 8-inch pie shell and bake for 7 minutes.
7. Reduce temperature to 350° and bake pie for an additional 45-55 minutes.

Chocolate Cherry
Pudding Cake

| Prep Time: 15 Minutes | Cook Time: 35-40 Minutes | Yield: 8-10 Servings |

It was Valentine's Day a few years back, and I was thinking about making something chocolatey and decadent. You know, the kind of cake that is so pretty you almost don't want to eat it, but in the end, just can't help yourself? Something rich and sweet that melts in your mouth? For me, nothing says "Valentine's Day" like chocolate and cherry. Perfect for showing someone just how much you love them!

Ingredients:

1 box of Devil's Food Cake Mix

½ cup Pecans, diced

½ cup Marachino Cherries, diced

10 Marachino Cherries, whole (for garnish)

6 tbsps Marachino Cherry Juice

8 oz Whipped Cream

3.4 oz box of Instant Chocolate Pudding Mix

3 Eggs, beaten

Process:

1. Preheat oven to 350°.
2. Mix all cake ingredients together in a bowl and fold cherries and nuts into the mix.
3. Cook instant pudding to package directions and put in the refrigerator.
4. Bake the cake for 35-40 minutes in a 23 cm deep cake pan. Take a toothpick and stick it into the cake to make sure it's cooked through. Set aside to cool.
5. Add the cherry juice to the whipped cream and fold in.
6. Top the cooled cake chocolate pudding. Then add cherry whipped cream and garnish with cherries.

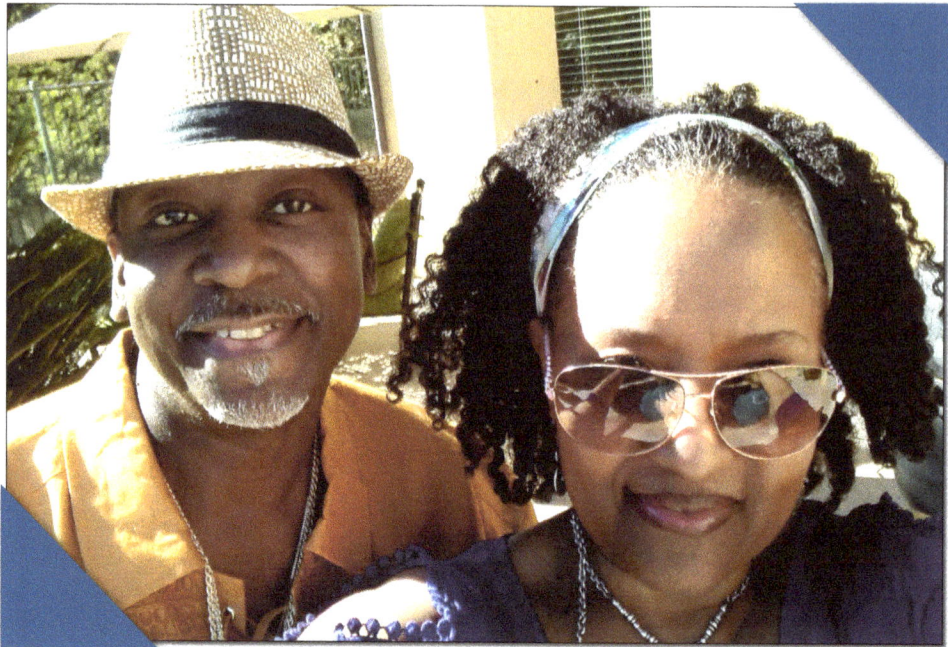

My dear friend, Janine, and me chilling before heading to the House of Blues for an evening of fun.

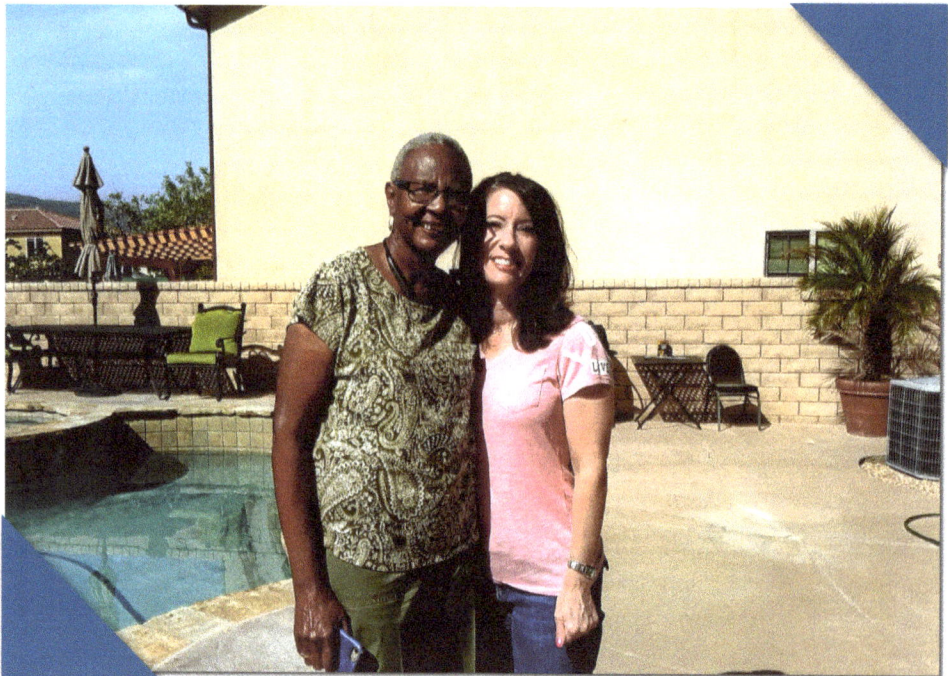

Moma Eve and Lynn relaxing by the pool in 2018. We were all just having fun, grilling, and swimming.

Moma Eve and me just having a wonderful day at the beach in 2018.

Banana
Pudding Cake

Prep Time: 15 Minutes	Cook Time: 25-30 Minutes	Yield: 8-10 Servings

Who doesn't love banana pudding? How about a banana pudding cake? I love cakes that are rich and creamy, and nothing is rich and creamy like banana pudding cake. This mouth-watering delicacy is perfect for company or just for you. I won't tell! Plus you can always say you're eating more fruit!

Ingredients:

1 box of Vanilla Wafer Cookies

1 box of Yellow Cake Mix

3 Eggs

2 tsps Vanilla Extract

2 large Bananas

1 small Lemon

8 oz Whipped Cream

3.4 oz box of Instant Vanilla Pudding Mix

1 tsp Banana Extract

Process:

1. Cook instant pudding to package directions and put in the refrigerator.

2. Preheat oven to 350°.

3. Cut the banana into slices and squeeze lemon juice over bananas. Set aside.

4. Combine cake ingredients and bake for 25-35 minutes in a 23 cm deep cake pan. Once it is done, remove it from the oven and let it cool.

5. Take your instant pudding and top the cake with it, spreading it evenly.

6. Add the banana extract to your tub of whipped cream and fold in.

7. Top the cake with the whipped cream and garnish with bananas and vanilla wafer cookies.

Meet the Chef
Billy Morris

BILLY MORRIS is a chef for Proctor & Gamble's headquarters in Cincinnati, Ohio, where he has worked for the last 39 years. He has been cooking for as long as he can remember and graduated from Scarlet Oaks Vocational School at the age of 17.

Billy has been a singer since he was 7 years old, but he also enjoys other creative endeavors such as modeling, drawing, painting, and interior design. In his free time, Billy loves spending time with his friends and family and attending live shows, but his favorite thing to do is make people smile. Billy is a lifelong lover of beautiful things, and he is thrilled to add this cook book to his collection.

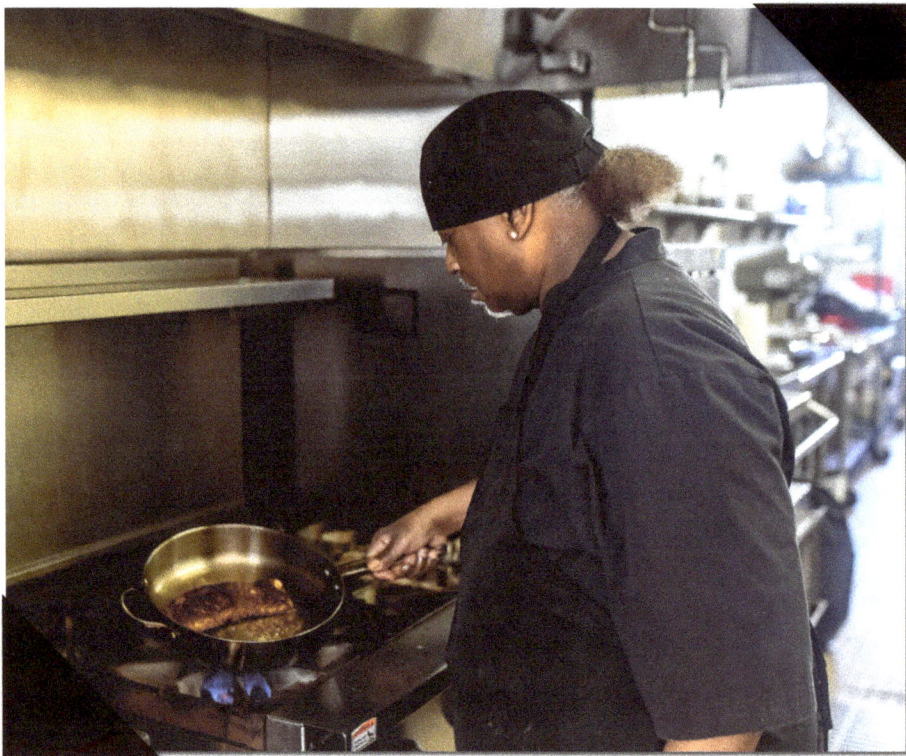

www.ingramcontent.com/pod-product-compliance
Lightning Source LLC
Chambersburg PA
CBHW040857100426

42813CB00015B/2825